SICKLE CELL ANEMIA

SICKLE CELL ANEMIA

George Beshore

A Venture Book

Franklin Watts

New York   Chicago   London   Toronto   Sydney

To Margaret

Photographs copyright ©: World Health Organization/National Library of
Medicine: p. 14; Photo Researchers, Inc./Science Photo Library: pp. 16 (Prof.
Marcel Bessis), 22 (Moredon Animal Health), 24 (Jackie Lewin, Royal Free
Hospital), 29 (NIBSC), 33 (Irving Geis/SS), 35 (Ken Eward/SS), 52 (Chuck
Brown); UPI/Bettmann: p. 18; Gamma-Liaison: pp. 21 (S. Peterson), 40
(P. Howell), 50 (Christian Vioujard); Sickle Cell Detection and Information
Program, Detroit, Mi.: p. 38; March of Dimes Birth Defects Foundation:
p. 44; Custom Medical Stock Photo: pp. 62 (Kevin Beebe), 65 (Peter Burndt,
M.D.), 73 (SIU); Wide World Photos: p. 74.

Library of Congress Cataloging-in-Publication Data

Beshore, George.
Sickle cell anemia / George Beshore.
p.   cm.—(A Venture book)
Includes bibliographical references and index.
ISBN 0—531-12510-6
1. Sickle cell anemia—Juvenile literature.   [1. Sickle cell anemia.
2. Diseases.] I. Title
RC641.7.S5B47 1994
616.1'527—DC20   94-15513   CIP   AC

CONTENTS

SICKLE CELL
ANEMIA

1
A LONG AND PAINFUL HISTORY

Most people have experienced the pain of a tooth-ache, or of a badly skinned knee, or of a bruised elbow. Some also know how frightening it is to have a stomachache or some other pain in their bodies that makes it necessary to go to a hospital.

Some children have to make frequent trips to the hospital starting when they are very young. Each visit is brought on by severe pains in their joints, in their stomachs, or in other parts of their bodies. They do not know how bad their agony will get, how long it will last, or what treatment they will need while they are there.

These children have sickle cell anemia, a disease that affects their blood. Sickle cell anemia is passed from one generation to the next, so it is hereditary. Sickle cell anemia is the most serious form of sickle cell disease.

Janet Brown* is a child with this disease. She was diagnosed as having sickle cell anemia when she was only two months old. Janet had her first severe attack of pain when she was one year old. At first she could

* Case histories are used with permission of the *Comprehensive Review*, a publication of the University of South Alabama Comprehensive Sickle Cell Center. The children's names have been changed.

not get out of bed. Then she couldn't walk, and she cried when she tried to stand up. "I knew from what the doctors had told me that it was the disease," her mother said.

A resident of Mobile, Alabama, Janet has problems that affect people all over the world who have sickle cell anemia. Like them, she often suffers from aches in her chest, sides, or hips. Sometimes these aches are so severe that she must go to a hospital emergency room.

Jacque Green, another Alabama resident, cannot remember when she was diagnosed with sickle cell anemia, but she knows that she has had it all her life. "You wish you could make the pain go away, because it hurts so badly," Jacque says. "Sometimes you can't even move or breathe."

Despite the pain, Jacque has gone on with her life, and she graduated from high school a few years ago. She did this even though, like others with this disease, she lives with constant feelings of fatigue.

THE GEOGRAPHY OF SICKLE CELL ANEMIA

Modern studies suggest that sickle cell anemia, the cause of Janet and Jacque's pain, probably originated thousands of years ago in or around the country now called Saudi Arabia. From there it spread east into India and west into Africa. Today areas of the world where sickle cell disease is found include Africa, the United States, Latin America and the Caribbean, India, Saudi Arabia, and some of the Mediterranean countries such as Italy and Greece. Although some people think that sickle cell disease affects only peo-

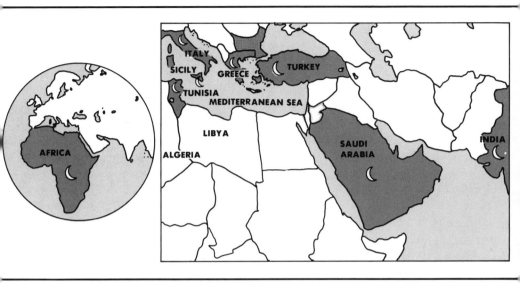

Areas of the world where the hereditary disease
of sickle cell anemia originated

ple of African descent, it affects people of other eth-
nic and geographic origins as well.

The impression that sickle cell disease affects
mostly people of African descent originates from the
knowledge that this ailment has been widespread in
tropical and subtropical areas of the world for centuries. There adults helplessly watched their children
die under mysterious circumstances. Unlike other
children who perished from starvation or from a
disease that left outward markings such as the scars of
smallpox, these young children seldom had anything
wrong with them that others could see. They just
went to sleep and never woke up. Even when such
children survived to be several years old, they often

11

developed puzzling symptoms. Some had swollen joints that hurt them badly; others suffered from severe internal pains. These children eventually died for no reason that others could understand.

"CHILDREN WHO COME AND GO"

In parts of Africa, many people decided that evil spirits must be causing the deaths. Special dances and chants were devised to drive these spirits away, but to no avail. Especially puzzling was the fact that most of the offspring born to certain couples died, while their neighbors' children were healthy.

One West African tribe had a special name for the children who died soon after being born into some families. They called them *ogbanjes*, which meant "children who come and go." These people believed that their ogbanje children kept on dying because an evil spirit was trying to be born into that particular family. They reasoned that each time the spirit attached itself to a child's soul, the baby died in order to protect the rest of the family from this demon. This superstition seemed to explain everything.

Scientists think that the inherited tendency toward sickle cell disease probably came to the New World with the first African slaves, because 20 or 25 percent of all Africans at that time are thought to have been carriers of the sickling trait.

According to this theory, sickle cell disease would have reached what is now the continental United States in 1619 when a Dutch ship landed at Jamestown, Virginia, with the first load of slaves. For the next three centuries, people of African descent and others in the United States—like those in other places around the world—continued to be troubled by the deaths of children who succumbed to infections and other complications because their bodies could not fight off invading diseases.

THE DISCOVERY OF SICKLE CELL ANEMIA

The true cause of these infant deaths, and the crippling pains suffered by other children who survived for a few years, remained a mystery until less than a hundred years ago. In 1904 James B. Herrick, a doctor working in a Chicago laboratory far from the tropics of Africa, began treating a twenty-year-old African-American man who had once lived on the West Indian island of Grenada. The man had *anemia*, a condition in which the blood cannot carry enough oxygen.

When Dr. Herrick studied the man's blood under a microscope, he expected to see tiny, round, red blood cells. He saw these, but he also observed curved and elongated cells. Each of these curved cells looked like the blade of a sickle. In 1910, after treating the man for about six years, Dr. Herrick published a report on what he concluded from his studies of the patient: here was a new condition. He called the condition sickle cell anemia.

Although other doctors, particularly those in the southern United States, had probably encountered patients with sickle cell anemia before, Dr. Herrick was the first to report his discovery in the medical literature. Soon other medical reports confirmed that these strange, sickle-shaped, red blood cells had something to do with the pain associated with the early childhood deaths.

*In 1910, Dr. James B. Herrick solved the
mystery surrounding the deaths of many infants
and children. Dr. Herrick, in examining a sample
of blood from an anemic patient under a microscope,
observed red blood cells curved like the blade of a
sickle. He called the condition sickle cell anemia.*

THE FORMS OF SICKLE CELL ANEMIA

During the next forty years many more observations about sickle cell anemia were reported. Doctors found that certain people had some sickle-shaped red cells in their blood but no symptoms. Next doctors discovered that people with these traits were carriers of sickle cell anemia without having its ill effects. This discovery explained why the parents of the African ogbanje children kept having babies who died even though they themselves seemed to be free of the disease.

Three forms of sickle cell anemia were identified in the 1920s. These were classified as "symptomless," "mild," and "severe." Since such terms were unscientific, scientists began to look for more specific designations. In 1926 Dr. T. P. Cooley and Dr. P. Lee, two researchers working together in Detroit, arrived at the classifications of the disease that are used today. Drs. Cooley and Lee classified the active form of the disorder as sickle cell anemia—the name that Dr. Herrick had used. They designated the form that produced mild or no symptoms *sickle cell trait*. Many reports during the next decade confused the two, but these terms were adopted by researchers and are still in use.

THE ROLE OF HEMOGLOBIN

Discoveries about the nature of sickle cell disease came rapidly after researchers sorted out the difference between the life-threatening form of the disease, sickle cell anemia, and the less-serious type, sickle cell trait. Around the middle of the twentieth

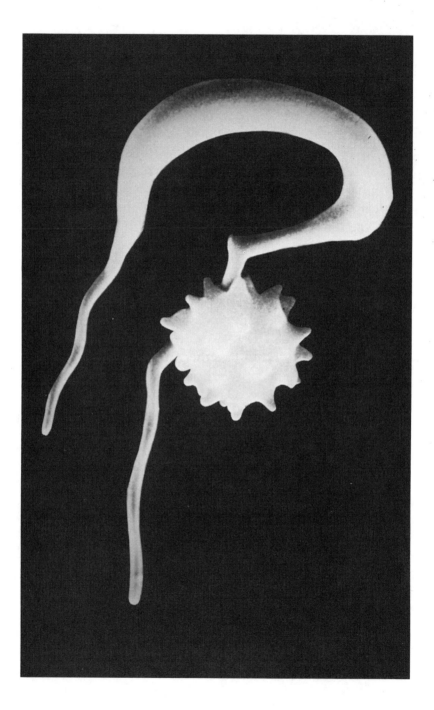

century, Dr. Linus Pauling, a distinguished chemist who later won the Nobel Prize twice for his work in chemistry and peace, made two important findings. In 1949 Dr. Pauling showed that an abnormal form of *hemoglobin*, a protein in the blood, causes the sickling phenomenon. Hemoglobin is the oxygen-carrying element in the blood's red cells.

Next Dr. Pauling demonstrated that blood from people with sickle-cell trait can be distinguished electrically from blood found in those who have the full-blown disease. Soon it was possible to test people for the two conditions by processing a few drops of a person's blood in an electric field to determine which type of hemoglobin was present. Such tests could be performed quickly and inexpensively.

THE DEVELOPMENT OF ELECTROPHORESIS

Within a few years, another scientist, Vernon Ingram, combined Dr. Pauling's tests with a chemical analysis to show the basic differences between normal and abnormal hemoglobin. Out of this work scientists developed a way to use a process called *electrophoresis* to test for both sickle cell anemia and sickle cell trait. Electrophoresis involves the movement of charged particles within an electric field under certain controlled conditions. In the case of

The long curving shape is a red blood cell that causes sickle cell anemia.

suspected sickle cell disease, a blood sample is prepared and placed in the instrument used for electrophoresis testing. Then an electric field is turned on. Electrically charged atoms of the different hemoglobins move toward the positively charged pole of the instrument at different speeds.

This method, when combined with additional chemical tests to further confirm the identity of the hemoglobin, allows a laboratory technician to quickly test for both sickle cell anemia and sickle cell trait.

The existence of the inactive form of the disease—sickle cell trait—explains why sickle cell anemia continues to be a major health problem today. Normally anyone who inherits a disease that kills many of its victims at a relatively young age will die without passing the condition on to his or her offspring. However, people with sickle cell trait do not suffer from the infections that kill so many people with the active form of the disease. As a result, people with sickle cell trait live normal lives, grow up, and have children of their own. These children then carry the inherited condition that produces either sickle cell trait or sickle cell anemia in future generations.

Dr. Linus Pauling at work at his kitchen table. Dr. Pauling, who has won the Nobel Prize for Chemistry and the Nobel Prize for Peace, discovered the cause of the sickling of the blood cells in the hemoglobin.

HOW MANY PEOPLE HAVE
SICKLE CELL DISEASE?

Today some 2.5 million Americans have some form of sickle cell disease. This figure includes African-Americans, Puerto Rican-Americans, and Greek- and Italian-Americans. Over 60,000 of these 2.5 million Americans have sickle cell anemia. The remainder have sickle cell trait or one of the variations of the disease. Most Americans with sickle cell anemia now survive, because treatment for the disease and its side effects is available.

Around the world, sickle cell anemia causes about 80,000 deaths each year, mostly in developing countries. In Africa, where the disease was once so widespread, the distribution is very uneven—from 0 to 60 percent of a population may have it.

SICKLE CELL ANEMIA AND MALARIA

Why did sickle cell anemia develop originally in the tropics and subtropics? We don't know the answer to that question, but we do know that very young children who have either sickle cell anemia or sickle cell trait are more resistant than other people to malaria, a serious disease that causes chills, high fever, and often death. More than one million people around

The Masai people in Africa are plagued by the disease of malaria. Here a doctor is examining a Masai patient who may have malaria.

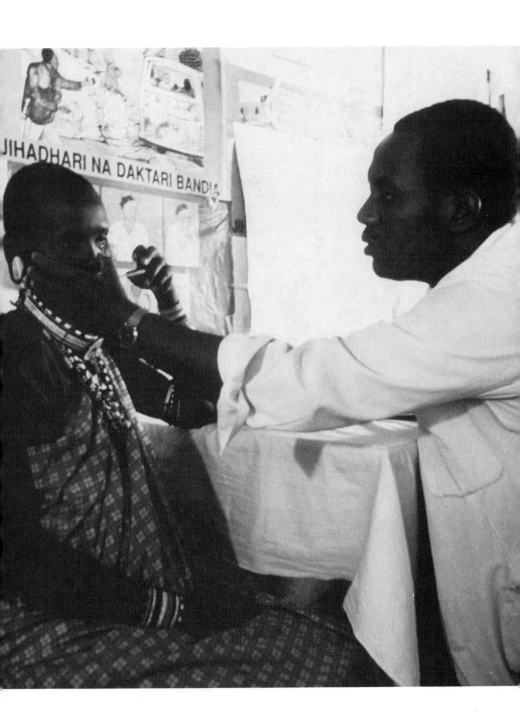

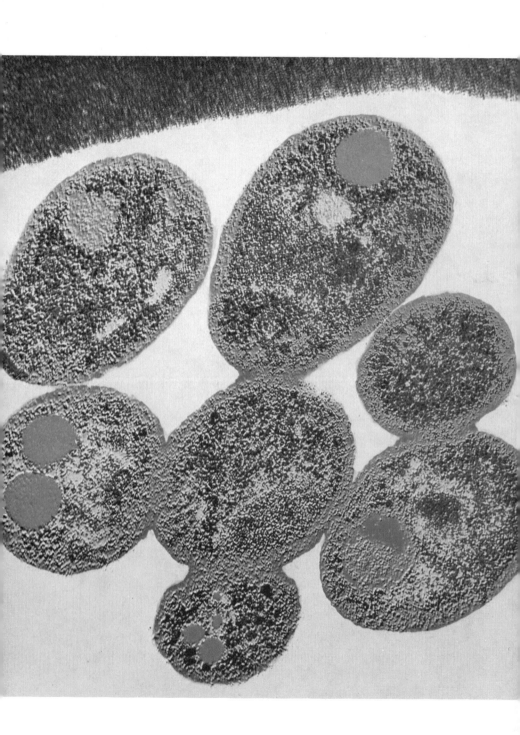

the world—most of them children under the age of five—still die each year from malaria, and the disease once killed far more people than that, mostly in the tropics.

Children with sickle cell disease are affected by malaria less severely and less frequently than children without sickle cell disease. The malaria germ is actually carried by one type of mosquito found in the tropics. When this mosquito bites an infected individual, the insect takes the malaria organism into its body with the blood that it sucks out. The malaria organism does not affect the mosquito, but the insect carries the germ around and may eventually pass it on to another person when the insect bites that individual. The malaria germ then circulates in the second person's bloodstream and produces the disease unless that individual's immune system can fight off the infection.

Scientists have found that the red blood cells of people with sickle cell disease break down quickly when the malaria germ attacks them. These cells are then discharged from the body before malaria can become firmly established in the individual's system.

A clump of merozoites, the infectious stage of the protozoan parasite that causes malaria. Each merozoite enters a human red blood cell, reproduces, and then releases the merozoites to infect other red blood cells. People with sickle cell are somewhat protected against malaria.

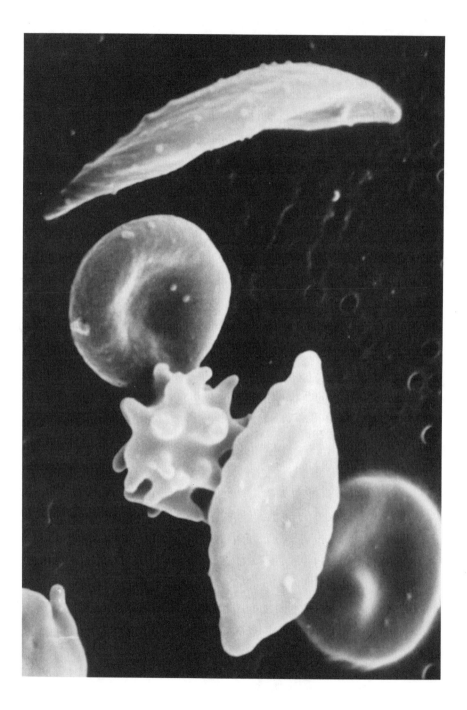

Those children who evaded death from malaria, and who lived long enough to reproduce, had offspring who (1) might have no symptoms of sickle cell disease, (2) might have sickle cell trait, or (3) might have full-blown sickle cell anemia. Depending upon their hereditary makeup, their children in turn either succumbed to malaria or sickle cell anemia or grew up to have their own children. Over time, the sickle cell gene spread in areas prone to malarial outbreaks, because of the protection it provided against that deadly malady.

Although sickle cell anemia is such a deadly disease, over the years the mechanism of evolution has "favored" its victims with anti-malarial protection in climates where malaria is prevalent. This doesn't explain why the sickle cell gene originated in the places it did, but it does explain why it found a foothold there.

Today malaria is under control in some areas where it once occurred in epidemic proportions, and in those areas the incidence of sickle cell disease has decreased, sometimes dramatically. This is because more children without immunity to malaria now grow up to have their own families, decreasing the

Several red blood cells:
(in descending order)
a sickled red blood cell;
a normal round red blood cell;
another abnormal red blood
cell (spiky); a red blood cell
that is beginning to sickle;
and a normal red blood cell.

percentage of people with sickle cell disease in the total population.

African-Americans may be most affected by sickle cell disease because of the way the disorder developed, but it is essential to keep in mind that there is absolutely no connection between skin color and sickle cell disease. This cannot be said often enough or strongly enough. Sickle cell disease affects people with dark skin color because the majority of people with dark skin either live in Africa or have ancestors who came from Africa.

Why nature conferred such a painfully mixed blessing on some people is not a question easily answered. But we can better understand this condition by learning more about it.

2

WHAT IS
SICKLE CELL ANEMIA?

Sickle cell anemia is a hereditary blood disorder that affects people in ways that can be felt and seen, such as causing pain and swelling. It also affects people in less obvious ways, including slowing physical development and damaging internal organs such as the liver, kidneys, and spleen. Later in life, sickle cell anemia may affect eyesight or cause strokes.

Most children with sickle cell anemia have symptoms that appear during the first four to six months of their lives, but a few children may have no symptoms until they are three or four years old. Doctors cannot predict exactly the course of the disease in each person.

Most people with sickle cell anemia spend a great deal of time in the hospital because of painful crises, as pain attacks are known. Most must also see their doctors frequently, because physicians need to watch for changes in their physical condition.

Sickle cell disease is not contagious in any of its forms. You cannot "get" it by contact with another person in any way, shape, or fashion—from touching them, from kissing them, from being sneezed on by them, by getting any of their blood on you, or by any similar means. The only way you can "get" any form of sickle cell disease is from one or both of your parents.

THE CIRCULATORY SYSTEM

Understanding sickle cell anemia requires knowledge of some key body processes. The heart pumps blood throughout the body. The right side of the heart sends blood to the lungs, which add oxygen and remove carbon dioxide. The blood then flows to the left side of the heart, which pumps it through the arteries to the rest of the body.

From the arteries, the blood is distributed to the organs and tissues through tiny, hairlike capillaries. Blood returns to the heart through the veins, and the process starts over again. The entire amount of blood in a person's body—five to six quarts— passes through the heart about once every minute.

A major function of the blood is to carry oxygen and nutrients to the body tissues and to take away waste products. Human blood consists of several parts. One is plasma, a straw-colored liquid that is about 90 percent water. The blood also has three kinds of cells plus other materials suspended in the fluid, including proteins, enzymes, and minerals such as salt and sugar.

The three kinds of blood cells are (1) platelets, which help stop bleeding; (2) white cells, which play an important role in defending the body against disease; and (3) red blood cells, which carry oxygen to the body tissues and take away carbon dioxide.

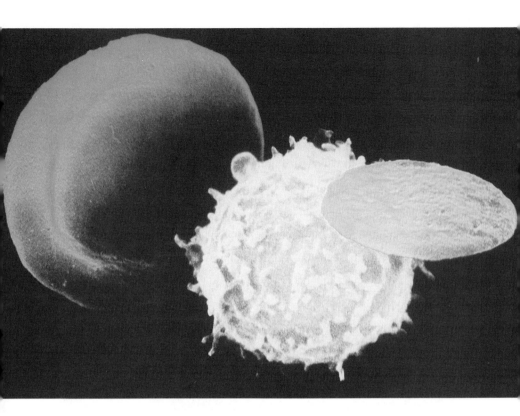

Three types of cells found in human blood: left, *a red blood cell that transports oxygen around the body;* center, *a white blood cell that is active in fighting infection;* right, *a blood platelet that controls blood clotting.*

THE ROLE OF RED BLOOD CELLS

Red blood cells give the blood its color because they contain the molecule hemoglobin, which Dr. Pauling studied in connection with sickle cell anemia. Hemoglobin in the red blood cells contains iron, which absorbs oxygen from the blood. In the tissues and organs, the oxygen is exchanged for carbon dioxide, which is taken back by the blood to the lungs and discharged from the body when a person exhales.

Red blood cells are produced in the bone marrow at a rate of 2 million to 10 million each second. At the same time, an equal number of exhausted red blood cells are broken down in body organs such as the liver and spleen, maintaining a delicate balance under normal conditions. The life span of a normal red blood cell is about 120 days; significantly less for cells affected by sickle cell anemia. The normal number of red blood cells for an adult male is about 5 million per cubic millimeter of blood. Adult females have about 500,000 fewer.

Normal red blood cells are round and flat, looking like tiny disks or doughnuts when viewed through a microscope. These cells are flexible, allowing them to squeeze through the tiny capillaries that connect the arteries and the veins. In these capillaries the red blood cells release their oxygen and take on carbon dioxide and other waste products.

If the body has too little hemoglobin or too few red blood cells, or if the ability of the hemoglobin in those cells to carry oxygen is reduced for any reason, anemia results. The symptoms of anemia are extreme tiredness and listlessness, whether the anemia results from sickle cell disease or from some other cause.

THE EFFECTS OF AN OXYGEN SHORTAGE ON THE BODY

There are several kinds of anemia, each dependent on what prevents the blood from carrying a sufficient supply of oxygen. One is sickle cell anemia, so named

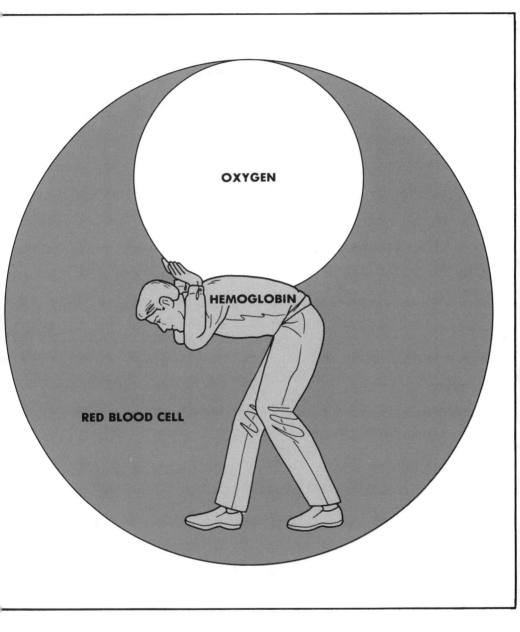

*Hemoglobin in the red blood cells
is the carrier of oxygen.*

because of the shape of the red blood cells. The hemoglobin molecules in the blood of people who have sickle cell anemia tend to release their oxygen too quickly. As the oxygen content drops, the cells become stiff and curve into the characteristic sickle shape that gives the disease its name. The fragility of sickled cells results in their short life span. With a shortage of red blood cells, anemia occurs.

When the red blood cells of a person with sickle cell anemia become stiff and rigid, they also tend to stick together and cannot squeeze through the capillaries. Blood flow is restricted, and body tissues become starved for oxygen.

Lack of oxygen causes a number of dangerous things to happen in the body. For one, cells may die. Internal organs then fail to function properly. Eventually the vital organs can fail. Sickled cells stuck together form blockages, which cause swelling and pain. Blockages are especially dangerous in parts of the body where the blood vessels are tiny, such as in the eyes and the internal organs. Impaired blood circulation in the joints causes them to become irritated and sore. If circulation fails in the brain, a crippling stroke can occur.

Cell death within the body also releases poisons into the system, causing problems that vary depending upon the parts of the body involved. Long before this happens, the body's cells begin to signal the lack of oxygen with pain. As the shortage of oxygen continues, the pain becomes more and more severe, resulting in a painful crisis.

The shortage of blood cells in vital organs greatly reduces the ability of the body to fight off infectious disease. Bacterial infections are 300 times higher in babies with sickle cell anemia than in normal infants.

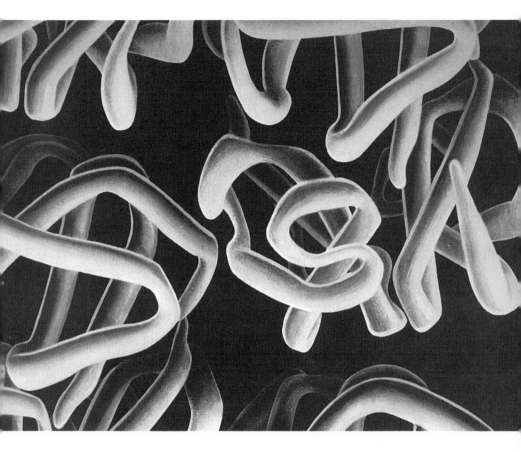

*Hemoglobin molecules in
sickle cell anemia*

THE SEVERITY OF THE DISEASE

The severity of sickle cell disease varies greatly, even between people in the same family. Part of the reason for this is that in people with sickle cell anemia not all the red blood cells sickle. If a lot of them sickle, the disease is much more serious than if fewer of them do.

People with sickle cell trait may have no symptoms of sickle cell anemia, or only mild ones—for example, occasional aches and pains. In a mild case of sickle cell anemia, the person might be tired a lot and feel generally under the weather. In more severe cases, the person is vulnerable to all kinds of infections; major organs can be affected; or excruciating pain and even death can occur.

In the past, perhaps half the people with sickle cell anemia lived to age twenty, and a few may have lived past age forty. New treatment programs greatly extend life spans today—at least in developed countries.

HEREDITY AND HEMOGLOBIN

Individuals with sickle cell disease have these complications because they have a different kind of hemoglobin from that of most people. Children inherit their hemoglobin type from their mothers and fathers, just as they do many other traits such as skin color, eye and hair color, body build, and basic intelligence. All inherited traits are carried by units in the body called genes.

Genes control the workings and development of our bodies and minds, and they are passed from one generation to the next. Every human being has millions of genes—there are about 10,000 in each body cell. A cell has two genes for every hereditary characteristic that the cell transmits. One gene comes from each of the child's parents. These two genes link up when a baby is conceived and produce the trait.

Most people have genes that instruct their bodies

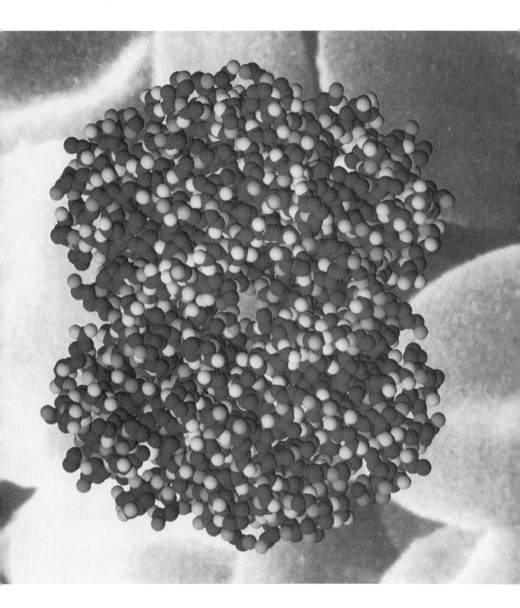

A computer-generated model of oxygenated human hemoglobin A against a background of red blood cells, the carriers of hemoglobin

to produce normal hemoglobin, called hemoglobin A. However, some have genes that result in abnormal forms of hemoglobin. One of these, called hemoglobin S, causes the sickling effect. This term—hemoglobin S—was coined in 1949 by Dr. Pauling, who first showed that this abnormal hemoglobin is present in people with sickle cell anemia.

A child who receives hemoglobin A genes from both parents will have hemoglobin A. This is designated with two *A*'s (AA) to show that both genes are of the A type. On the other hand, a child who receives hemoglobin S from both parents will have sickle cell anemia. This combination is designated SS—meaning one S gene from each parent. A child who inherits an A gene from one parent and an S gene from the other has a combination (AS) and has the sickle cell trait. People with sickle cell trait have enough normal hemoglobin in their blood to avoid the problems caused by sickle cell anemia, but they can pass on the disease to their children.

Sickle cell anemia develops in an average of one out of four children parented by two carriers of the sickle cell trait. The word "average" is used because one couple with sickle cell trait may have two or more children with sickle cell anemia while another such couple has none.

What happens when a person with normal hemoglobin marries a person with sickle cell trait? On average, half of the offspring they produce will have sickle cell trait. The chart on the facing page shows why these and other averages occur.

Other forms of sickle cell disease also exist. One is called sickle cell SC because it involves one gene (C) that is slightly different from the regular sickle cell gene (S). This form tends to be less severe than

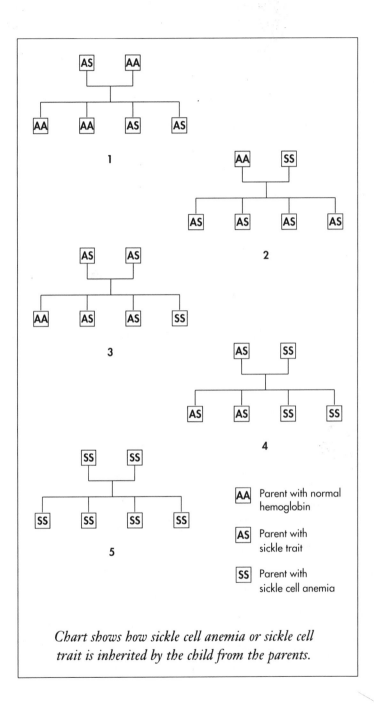

Chart shows how sickle cell anemia or sickle cell
trait is inherited by the child from the parents.

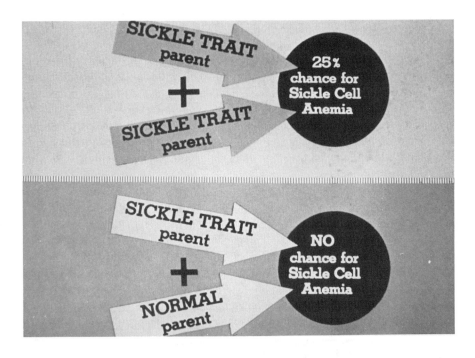

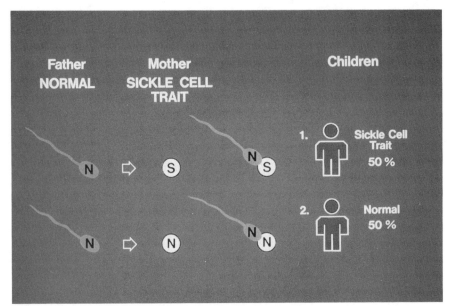

sickle cell anemia, and children with this disorder may reach late childhood before they notice the symptoms associated with sickle cell anemia.

Another form of the disease is sickle cell thalassemia (often abbreviated SC thal), which involves a gene of that name and a gene for sickle cell trait. SC thal is generally less severe than the main form of either sickle cell anemia or thalassemia.

Children with any of these forms of sickle cell disease need to be tested at an early age, and treatments need to be started as soon as possible. Testing and treatment costs money, as does the research needed to find new ways to control or stamp out sickle cell disease. To meet these needs, a national sickle cell program was started twenty years ago.

THE NATIONAL SICKLE CELL CONTROL ACT

While scientists such as Drs. Pauling, Cooley, and Lee were developing ways to test for sickle cell anemia, other health workers began emphasizing the

Top: *If both parents carry the sickle trait, there is a 25 percent chance that their child will develop sickle cell anemia. If one parent has normal hemoglobin, there is no chance that the child will develop sickle cell anemia, whether the other parent has the sickle trait, as shown here, or sickle cell anemia.* Bottom: *If one parent has normal hemoglobin and the other has the sickle trait, there is a 50 percent chance that their child will have the sickle trait and a 50 percent chance that their child will be normal.*

need to establish a national sickle cell disease program. This call for action was echoed by the National Institutes of Health, a number of children's hospitals, and other medical organizations.

Bills were introduced into Congress, but legislation to establish such a program was unsuccessful until May, 1972, when Congress passed the National Sickle Cell Anemia Control Act. This law established a national program to combat sickle cell disease, including comprehensive centers to work with state and local institutions on sickle cell disease education and research. The act also established clinics to screen children and help those with sickle cell anemia get proper care.

When the original National Sickle Cell Anemia Control Act expired in 1975, some congressional leaders suggested that the program be incorporated under a larger, more general bill covering other genetic diseases, and this was done.

Today the comprehensive centers established by the original sickle cell disease act continue to work with individuals and state government programs, as well as with national, regional, and local organizations. Together these organizations provide information and help people with sickle cell disease.

Michael Wilburn is a researcher of sickle cell anemia. As a result of researchers' efforts, new treatments have been discovered for people suffering with the hereditary disease.

3

INFANTS AND YOUNG CHILDREN WITH SICKLE CELL ANEMIA

Some of the most serious effects of sickle cell disease are felt within a few months after birth. Symptoms at this age include irritability, fever, frequent colds, pale nails, yellow eyes, and painful swelling of the hands and feet. Many infants need special care at that time in order to survive the danger of infection, which is great. For this reason, doctors need to detect the disease as early as possible and begin preventive procedures.

Sickle cell disease can be detected before birth through amniocentesis, a process that involves withdrawing and testing the fluid that surrounds the unborn baby while the fetus is still in the mother's body. If doctors find that a child will be born with sickle cell anemia, the parents then must decide whether they want to terminate the pregnancy. If the mother and father decide to let the pregnancy continue, they can also begin preparing to deal with the medical condition as soon as the child is born.

An alternative to amniocentesis for prenatal diagnosis is a process called chorionic villus sampling (CVS). A woman who is less than eleven weeks pregnant should be informed about CVS. This method has been used by many women during the ninth

A student in a New York City high school
is being screened for sickle cell anemia.

through eleventh weeks of pregnancy, but it cannot be used for everyone.

Chorionic villi are part of the tissues that surround the fetus and eventually become the placenta, or afterbirth. A small sample is removed using a catheter (a thin tube) inserted through the vagina into the uterus under ultrasound guidance. Results are usually available in one to three weeks.

Screening of newborn babies to detect sickle cell anemia, along with other inherited conditions, is an important part of the sickle cell disease program in forty-two states, the District of Columbia, and Puerto Rico. As of December 1990, the only states without newborn screening programs for sickle cell anemia were Alaska, Hawaii, Idaho, Maine, Montana, North Dakota, Oregon, and South Dakota.

Screening of newborn babies is done by taking blood from the infant's heel or from the umbilical cord that connects the baby with its mother before and during birth. The sample is then screened by the electrophoretic technique described earlier.

PREVENTING INFECTION

Infants who test positive for sickle cell anemia are put on daily doses of penicillin soon after birth. This medication does not affect the disease but prevents the infections that took so many lives in the past. Before doctors began to use penicillin treatments as a preventive measure, up to 30 percent of all children with sickle cell anemia died before they were three years old. Many of these deaths occurred when babies were only a few months old. One of the killers was a bacteria that causes pneumonia. Another was salmonella, also a bacteria.

One factor in these early deaths from infection is the effect of sickle cell anemia on the child's spleen, an organ that plays a major role in the body's defenses against infection. By blocking tiny blood vessels in the spleen, sickle cell anemia keeps this organ from functioning as it normally would to fight disease. Sickle cell anemia also lowers the amount of certain disease-fighting proteins in an individual's blood, adding to the disease problem.

THE VALUE OF PENICILLIN

The value of using penicillin to prevent early childhood infections was dramatically demonstrated by a study conducted nearly twenty years ago by the National Institutes of Health in Bethesda, Maryland. The research involved over 200 children with sickle cell anemia, all less than three years old. Approximately half were given penicillin twice a day; the others received a fake dosage, called a placebo.

A dramatic drop in cases of infection occurred among the group that received the real penicillin. The rate of infection fell by 84 percent, and many lives were saved. Within eighteen months the benefits of the medical procedure were so obvious that the study was ended early.

Since that time, the use of penicillin for infants with sickle cell anemia has become standard practice. It is continued until the child is at least three years old—sometimes until the age of five or beyond, depending upon a doctor's recommendation in each case. Penicillin can be injected into the infant's bloodstream, but the preferred treatment is a relatively low dose in fluid form that can be drunk twice a day. Studies indicate that children seldom build up immunity against the antibiotic when it is given this way. If a child is allergic to penicillin, other antibiotics are used.

THE SIDE EFFECTS OF MEDICATION

Care givers must watch for side effects, such as a rash or vomiting, that indicate an allergic reaction to penicillin, especially at the beginning of the treatment.

The medication also must be given twice a day without fail. Doctors recommend that one person in the home be responsible for seeing that the child receives his or her medication. Otherwise family members may assume that others have given the medicine, and doses may be missed. Such errors can be fatal.

The regularity of medication times can cause problems in families where both parents work outside the home. Just keeping a supply on hand can also be a challenge, because it is generally possible to stock only a two-week supply of penicillin at a time. Otherwise the drug loses its strength.

Frequent examinations help doctors discover low-grade fevers or other signs of infection. Physicians can also detect changes in the child's physical condition, including minor swelling in the joints that might otherwise go unnoticed. Doctors may also find changes in internal organs that can signal dangerous complications. Such changes often escape the attention of untrained persons.

CHOOSING A PHYSICIAN

Children with sickle cell anemia need to see the same physician each time they visit the doctor's office. This is important, because cases vary greatly. A doctor familiar with the patient's history will be able to detect small changes and know which may be significant. If a parent's health insurance requires trips to clinics where the choice of doctors is restricted, this can become a problem. Lack of health insurance and lack of nearby medical facilities are other problems for many parents of children with sickle cell anemia.

The wide variations in care needed by different

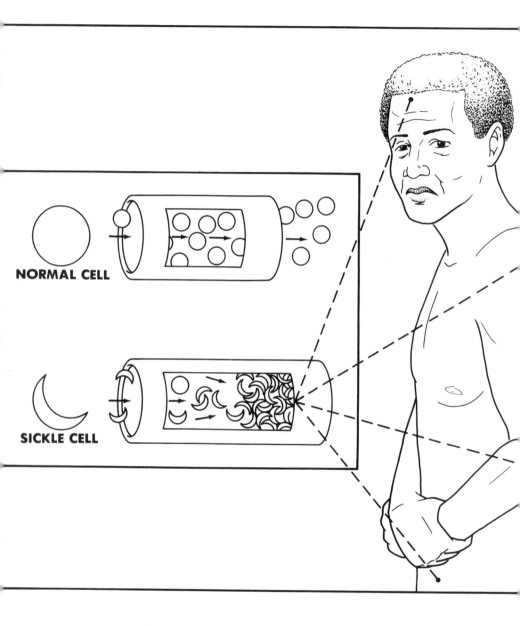

NORMAL CELL

SICKLE CELL

*Sickle cells that stick together block the blood vessels and
cause swelling and pain at certain points in the body.*

infants with sickle cell disease can be confusing. For example, some patients are admitted to the hospital as frequently as once a month in the first two or three years of life; others may not have to be hospitalized for several years. Some may have frequent incidents of swelling and soreness of the joints due to blockage of circulation; others may have little trouble along this line.

Hospital admissions due to painful crises occur when the sickle-shaped cells clog up small blood vessels of a child's internal organs. Such pain tells the person that serious problems are involved. Often a doctor's examination is needed to determine just exactly what is happening within the body and the best course of action to relieve the pain. Pain killers may be needed. Common, non-narcotic kinds such as aspirin and acetaminophen can be enough, or stronger medications such as morphine-based drugs may be needed.

BLOOD TRANSFUSIONS

Although it is important to alleviate pain with medication, care must be taken that the treatment doesn't simply reduce the pain with pills when a more complete diagnosis is needed to prevent damage to internal organs. Blood transfusions are frequently the only way that a doctor can relieve the basic condition creating the pain. Transfusions are especially useful when a child's red blood cell count is low. These treatments increase the number of red cells, boosting the oxygen-carrying capacity of the blood. Transfusions also lower the concentration of sickle cells and

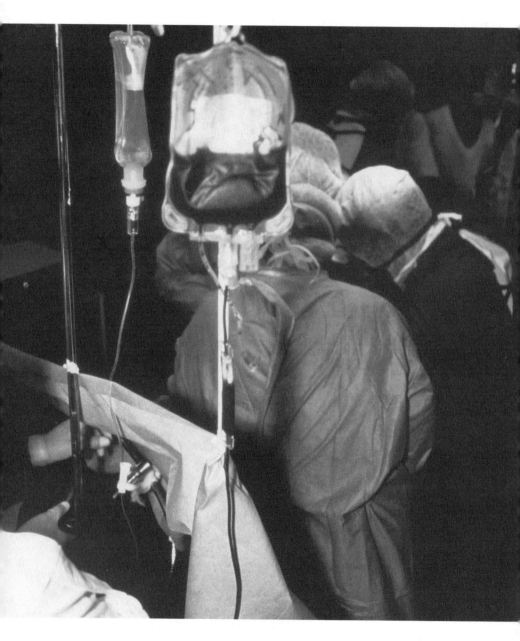

A blood transfusion

reduce the tendency of these cells to stick together. Blood transfusions are indicated when there are high concentrations of sickle cells in an internal organ. Transfusions are also indicated in life-threatening situations where there is a risk of stroke or acute lung problems. This treatment is not used for uncomplicated painful episodes or minor infections.

Danger exists that the blood given in a transfusion may be infected with hepatitis and other viral diseases, but these risks are no greater for sickle cell patients than they are for others who need transfusions. In recent years people have been concerned about getting AIDs from blood transfusions, but safeguards now exist to keep this deadly disease out of the nation's basic blood supply.

THE PATIENT'S ROLE

The child and his or her parents can take precautions to reduce the frequency of painful incidents, and both the child and the family need to be aware of these. Dehydration—lack of fluids in the body—is a major cause of painful complications. Exposure to cold often brings on a painful crisis.

As children become old enough to understand what is happening when these painful episodes occur, they can often be taught how to avoid them. Boys and girls can learn to pay special attention to their fluid intake and to dress warmly when going outside on cold days. Most people with sickle cell anemia also need to avoid excessive physical exertion, a requirement that is often difficult for active children.

Few children can avoid painful crises entirely, so

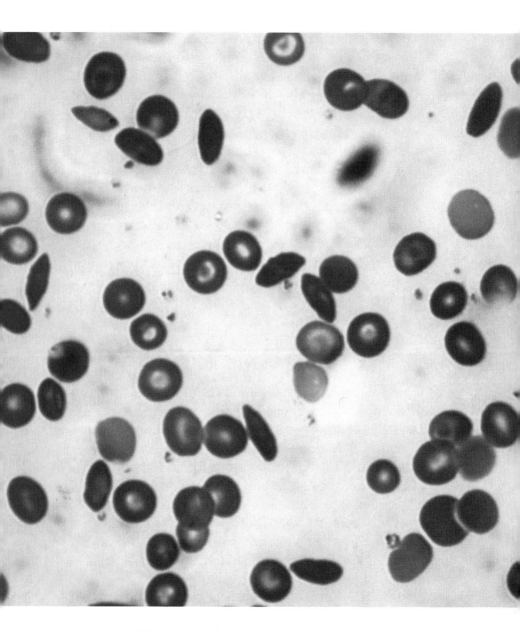

*Blood smear of a person with sickle cell
anemia. Note the sickle shape of some cells.*

learning to distinguish between pain that can be handled by home remedies and pain that requires professional medical attention becomes essential. Young children often have difficulty understanding why they must abide by special rules that don't apply to their playmates and friends. They may also wonder why they have these painful times when their friends seem to be free from them.

Helping young children understand the nature of their disease is important during early childhood. It will also aid them when they enter school and find out that other children do not have to cope with the same problems that they are facing.

The way that sickle cell anemia can affect young people's activities—and the things that families can do—are illustrated by the lives of two girls who have this disease.

TWO SISTERS

Five-year-old Bettina and seven-year-old Carrie are sisters.* They both wear Medic Alert bracelets that read "Sickle Cell Anemia." When her classmates ask about the bracelet, Carrie says, "It's to help the doctors and nurses take care of me when I get sick. I have sickle cell anemia. That's got to do with my blood cells—the red ones. Sometimes they change shape from round into long and pointed, and then I feel tired and sometimes I get a stomachache."

Mrs. B., the girls' mother, is a registered nurse who understands their condition and the kind of care

* Bettina and Carrie are real girls. Their names have been changed.

they must have. She says, "Bettina and Carrie have the most serious kind of sickle cell anemia, and yet the disease doesn't give them many problems. Bettina has had the worse time of it. She has a problem about every three months."

Since she was born, Bettina has had to be hospitalized six times so doctors could treat the infection and pain that troubles people with sickle cell.

Mrs. B. points out that with proper care, children with sickle cell anemia have few problems. Each day, Bettina and Carrie take two penicillin tablets and one folic acid pill. The sickle-shaped cells interfere with the body's ability to fight infection, and the penicillin is needed to help fight infection. The folic acid helps the body make more red blood cells. Mrs. B. says, "While I know they don't always do it, the girls should drink a glass of water or juice every hour. This keeps the blood flowing well, which prevents clumping of sickle cells in the blood vessels." Mrs. B. adds, "They tire easily and should take a five-minute rest after half-an-hour of exercise."

The B. family lives in New England, and Mrs. B. has one firm rule about winter weather. She says, "When the girls go out in winter weather, even for a minute, they must bundle up—coats, boots, hats, gloves, everything. And even then, I don't like them to stay out more than half an hour. The cold causes the blood vessels to constrict, which can bring on a pain crisis." To this she adds, "Beyond these rules, I try to let them live like typical children." And for the most part, they do.

Both Carrie and Bettina are thin and tall for their ages. They wear their hair in short Afros like their mother. Carrie loves to cook. Bettina is Carrie's assistant and chief sampler in the kitchen. Bright and inquisitive, Carrie was the valedictorian of her kindergarten class. She is easygoing and well liked by her fellow second-graders. "In school, everyone wants to be my partner," says Carrie. Her ambition is to be a doctor.

Bettina is a shy and friendly girl. She has learned her alphabet and can write her name. Her ambition is to have a cat and dog.

As on other typical days, the B. family rose at seven. Breakfast was pancakes and sausage. As she ate her breakfast, Carrie remembered to take her penicillin. "Don't forget your juice," said Mrs. B. Carrie drank her juice and then rushed to get ready for the school bus. Today was special. For days she had worked on a composition about a boy and a dog. It was her first big test in writing. Today the teacher would hand the papers back. Carrie was anxious to see what her grade would be. As she rushed out the door, Mrs. B. said, "Don't forget to drink your water . . . and don't forget your rest breaks."

The first class was reading, Carrie's favorite. On this day, she learned three new words—elephant, Africa, and giraffe. Next came computer class. Carrie tried out her new words on the computer. When she spelled elephant correctly, a drawing of the animal appeared on the screen. Then the teacher handed out the compositions. At the top of Carrie's was a big red *A*. Carrie was proud. "Wait till mommy sees this," she thought.

Gym was next, and Carrie rushed off to change into her gym shorts. On the way she realized she had left her composition on her desk. She rushed back to get it and then hurried to the locker room.

"Today, children, we're going to start off with a dance. Join hands and form a circle," said Mrs. Foley, the gym teacher. As the music played, the children danced around in a circle. Then Mrs. Foley turned off the music and said, "Now, everyone, form rows, now raise your arms, lower them, hands on hips, sway side to side, raise one knee, then the other."

As she raised her knee, Carrie's stomach began to hurt. Because she had rushed back for her paper, she had not had time to drink some water. She stopped and put her hands to her stomach. Mrs. Foley said, "All right, class, take a five-minute rest."

The teacher came over to Carrie and said, "Forgot your water, didn't you?" Carrie nodded. "Why don't you go across the hall to the nurse's office," the teacher suggested. After a short rest on the nurse's cot and a big drink of water Carrie felt much better.

At lunch, Carrie made sure she got the liquids that she needed. She also had soup and gelatin. After lunch came math and music. When the dismissal bell rang, Carrie joined some classmates in a soccer game. She remembered to drink some more water first. After about half an hour, Carrie began to feel tired and sat down for a five-minute rest.

By four o'clock, Carrie was home. "Mommy's going to be late," said Mr. B. "She's got a meeting and then has to pick up Bettina. Let's surprise her and get dinner ready. We'll make your favorite dinner. I'll make the macaroni and cheese, and you make pigs-in-the-blanket."

Bettina's day began just as Carrie's had— pancakes and sausage, a big glass of juice, and a penicillin pill. Then Mr. B. took her to a day-care center. At day care, Bettina practiced writing her name. Then she began drawing a picture of her family. In the middle were her mother and father, and on one side were her big brother, Davie, and her big sister, Carrie. On the other side she drew herself and a large, brown dog. They didn't have a dog, but Bettina knew that some day they would get one.

After lunch Bettina felt an ache in her leg. The ache got worse. Mrs. Jennings, who was in charge of the day-care center, gave Bettina a Tylenol-codeine tablet. The pain went away. But by 5:30, when Mrs. B. came to pick up Bettina, the pain was back. "Both legs hurt, Mommie. Please carry me—I can't walk," Bettina said through her tears.

At home, Mrs. B. gave Bettina more Tylenol-codeine, but the pain didn't go away. Mrs. B. massaged Bettina's legs, hoping to ease the clogging of sickled cells in the blood vessels. Bettina refused her favorite dinner of macaroni and cheese and pigs-in-the-blanket. "At least drink some juice and take your pill," said Mrs. B.

By early evening, Bettina was whimpering with pain. "I don't want it to hurt anymore," she said. Finally, at nine o'clock, Mrs. B. decided to call the doctor. He told her to meet him at the hospital emergency room.

Bettina spent the next five days in the hospital. Thin, plastic tubes fed fluids and morphine into her veins. Gradually the pain got better, and Bettina soon felt well enough to watch her favorite television programs.

Says Mrs. B.: "Bettina has a pain crisis like this about every three months. But she usually doesn't have to go to the hospital. On the other hand, Carrie has few problems. I am very careful to make sure they follow the rules. And yet Bettina has more problems than Carrie."

Bettina and Carrie both have this advice for other children with sickle cell anemia: "Drink a lot. It doesn't have to be water—popsicles, jello, soup, soda—they all count. And be sure to take your penicillin."

4

GROWING UP AND LIVING WITH SICKLE CELL DISEASE

When children approach school age, parents face the sometimes difficult decision of turning their offspring over to caregivers who are outside the home. Although some parents want to keep at home youngsters whom they consider to have a physical impairment, healthy development is possible only if children with sickle cell anemia are allowed to live as nearly normal lives as possible.

This means that as soon as these children reach school age, they should be enrolled in regular classroom work. However, parents need to tell the appropriate school officials of their child's condition. Written information about each individual's condition, to be shared with the teacher and school nurse, may be helpful, as is a letter from the patient's doctor explaining some of the basic facts about sickle cell anemia. These facts would include the point that, since the disease is not contagious, teachers need not worry about contact between the child with sickle cell anemia and his or her classmates. Of course, general information on sickle cell anemia is also provided to schools by health centers and national organizations.

PARENTAL GUILT

Often fathers or mothers of a child with sickle cell disease feel guilty for having brought the child into the world. Parents may blame themselves for their child's troubles. Guilt can be a real problem for a parent with sickle cell trait, who may blame himself or herself for the child's disease.

Sometimes the parents realize that they have such feelings, but more often they bury their thoughts and feelings. When these thoughts and feelings are buried, people often have difficulty dealing with their anger and frustration because they fail to recognize their source.

Children with sickle cell disease often have unrecognized feelings of fear, resentment, or self-pity. Fear of pain, especially when it has been frequent and drastic during childhood, may remain long after the severity of such episodes is gone. Lingering questions such as "Why is this happening to me?" may haunt a child, and later the adult.

Expert counseling is designed to bring such thoughts and feelings to the surface so that the people who have them can make honest efforts to deal with their emotions on an intelligent, rational basis.

PROBLEMS OF SIBLINGS

Brothers and sisters of a patient with sickle cell anemia may feel shame, often without realizing the source of such feelings. In other cases siblings may resent the special attention that parents give to the child. For this reason, the entire family may need counseling.

Children with sickle cell disease, as well as their families, often feel isolated, thinking that their problems make them different from their friends or neighbors. For this reason a support group can be helpful, allowing the individual with sickle cell anemia to meet others who have the same condition, learn about community resources, and deal with these problems. Support groups also exist for parents of children with sickle cell disease, and these can be extremely helpful.

THE ROLE OF TEACHERS

Teachers should know that fatigue can be a problem for children with sickle cell anemia. When children with sickle cell anemia occasionally put their heads down on the desk to rest, they are simply following their bodys' commands to combat the fatigue factor that is a part of their disease.

Teachers also need to know about the possibility of a painful crisis at any time and what to do on such occasions in terms of notifying the parents or a family physician. In addition, teachers need to be told that a child with sickle cell anemia does not need to be treated differently from other growing children except when a painful crisis occurs.

Maintaining a normal lifestyle for school-age children helps them develop positive attitudes toward the world and build positive self-images. Many children with sickle cell disease have successfully attended summer camps, some for children with special needs, others for children without them. School and summer camp activities foster independence and provide a child with an opportunity to feel more

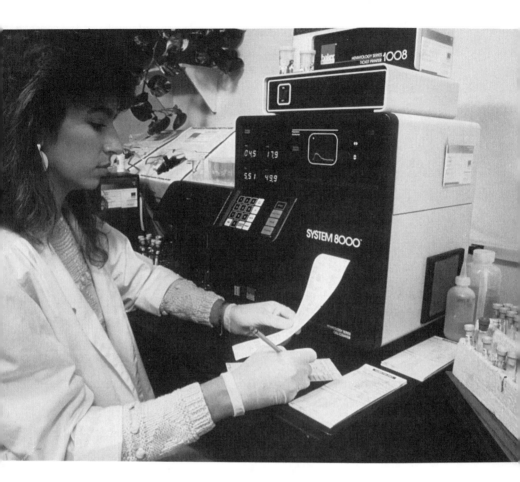

Medical records that are shared with the school can alert teachers to ways they can help children with sickle cell anemia.

like his or her peers and more able to do similar things. Overprotection by parents, family, friends, or teachers can pose serious problems for children, especially those approaching their adolescent years, who want to be independent and need freedom to act on their own.

ADOLESCENCE

As young people with sickle cell anemia enter their adolescent years, special problems may develop, including slower-than-normal growth and delayed sexual development. These may cause teenagers much distress, because at that age most young people don't like to be different from their friends. Fortunately, neither problem tends to be permanent. Instead teenagers with sickle cell anemia just may reach normal stages a few years later than their friends and acquaintances.

Teen participation in sports depends upon the individual case. Frequently teens with sickle cell anemia need to be able to set their own pace when participating in an activity such as swimming, tennis, or basketball. This means stopping to rest when necessary to avoid becoming overtired. Competitive, demanding sports may be suitable for some children but not for others with these restrictions.

Although many people with sickle cell anemia lead normal lives for many years, others develop complications due to the blockage of circulation within a specific organ, such as the gallbladder. There a blockage often leads to development of gallstones, which occur in about 14 percent of children with sickle cell anemia before they are ten years old. Thirty percent of all adolescents with sickle cell anemia have gallstones, and as many as 75 percent of adults will suffer from them by age thirty. Gallstones may cause few if any problems for years—or they may produce nausea, vomiting, and pain. Surgery is usually deferred until pain occurs.

Liver problems, caused by blocked veins in that organ, frequently include jaundice, which produces a yellowish coloring in the eyes and sometimes fever. Blood transfusions, so often necessary in managing sickle cell anemia, sometimes cause enlargement of the liver.

KIDNEY AND URINARY TRACT PROBLEMS

The kidneys are another area where tiny blood vessels are found, so sickle cell anemia also frequently causes circulation blockages. Kidney malfunction can result in serious complications. Urinary tract infections and high blood pressure also can occur.

Leg ulcers occur in between 10 and 20 percent of patients with sickle cell anemia. They usually appear between the ages of ten and fifty and are seen more frequently in males than in females. Active patient participation in the care of leg ulcers is essential, because these sores need to be washed and treated with the right surface medications.

Painful joints in the legs and elsewhere throughout the body are common in people with sickle cell anemia. This condition is caused by poor blood supply to the areas around the joints, leading to tissue death in these places.

The reduced oxygen-carrying capacity of the blood due to any form of anemia places extra demands on the heart. The resulting increased output can have harmful side effects. The eyes also contain tiny blood vessels and can be adversely affected by sickle cell anemia. These and other complications of sickle cell anemia emphasize the need for patients to continue to have regular physical checkups throughout their lives.

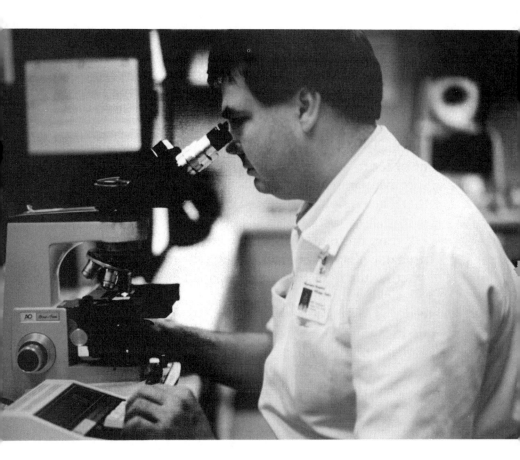

Examining specimens of blood for signs of anemia

GOING OUT INTO THE ADULT WORLD

Adults with sickle cell anemia will pretty much carry on from where they were when they were teenagers. They may have the same medical problems they had when they were adolescents or children, or they may be affected with new complications. As they go out into the world, they will face new situations that will test their bodies as well as their minds.

Teens and adults of childbearing age have special considerations. Sickle cell anemia carries some increased risks for potential mothers and their fetuses but does not in itself prohibit pregnancies. Young women need to seek medical care early in pregnancy in order to be closely monitored. Both of the prospective parents should have blood tests, as the father's hemoglobin type needs to be identified along with that of the mother. If both parents have sickle cell trait, this increases the need to consider having a prenatal diagnosis (amniocentesis) to determine whether the fetus has sickle cell anemia.

Sickle cell anemia also presents a number of social and psychological challenges for patients and their families. Good counseling can help both the patient and his or her parents cope with such problems as they arise during childhood and adolescence. Some of these challenges will involve the patient directly. Others concern the parents or other family members, such as brothers and sisters.

Most occupations can be pursued, but some, involving great physical demands, may not be possible. Being a test pilot or an Antarctic explorer may not be in the cards, but there is no reason why people with sickle cell anemia whose medical advisers approve, can't try to do what they want to do and be what they want to be.

DISCRIMINATION

In 1909, at the first meeting of the National Association for the Advancement of Colored People, scientists presented evidence proving that African-Americans were not physically or mentally inferior to whites. One contention of racists had been that African-Americans should not have full rights of American citizenship because they did not have the physical or mental ability to use those rights. Over the years African-Americans claimed their rights, and those old beliefs about inferiority have died away.

As more knowledge about sickle cell disease emerged, however, fears mounted in African-American communities across the nation that sickle cell anemia might be used to discriminate against African-Americans seeking jobs, insurance, and higher education. Some African-Americans regarded the new publicity about the disease with shame and suspicion. Others saw sickle cell as new ammunition for racists to use in order to discriminate against them.

For the most part, African-American concerns focused on sickle cell trait. Approximately 20 percent of African-Americans have the trait. People with this condition do not suffer the symptoms of sickle cell anemia, a fact disputed by some scientists in 1970. As a result, African-Americans with the trait were being discriminated against in certain situations.

In 1970 an army doctor, Major Richard A. Binder, published a report in a medical journal that attributed the deaths of four army recruits in 1968 and 1969 to sickle cell trait. The four recruits had collapsed and died during strenuous basic training at Fort Bliss. The army base, near El Paso, Texas, is 4,060 feet above sea level. Major Binder contended that the recruits died because their blood cells sickled during strenuous exercise at high altitude. He pointed out that an autopsy revealed that all of the victims had severely sickled red blood cells.

Several years later, an Air Force doctor reported that two African-American Air Force Academy cadets collapsed and died during strenuous exercise at the Academy in Colorado Springs, which is also at a high altitude.

In another study reported in 1973, thirty-four African-American professional football players were found to have sickle cell trait. The researchers concluded that the condition did not interfere with athletic ability and that people with sickle cell trait could engage in strenuous exercise.

That same year the National Academy of Sciences, after studying the available information, issued a recommendation that African-Americans with sickle cell trait be barred from serving as pilots or copilots. Immediately the Air Force Academy banned people with the trait from admission. (People with sickle cell trait had been banned from flight training since the late 1940s.)

Finally, in 1980, retired Air Force flight surgeon Vance A. Marchbanks reported on a survey of 154 African-American pilots who had served during and after World War Two. Ten pilots were found to have had sickle-cell trait. The ten had logged flying hours ranging from 400 to 7,160 in unpressurized planes without incident, even though available oxygen in the planes was very low. In his paper, Marchbanks noted that in 1974 the Department of Defense had urged that more medical studies be done to follow up on the 1973 NAS recommendation.

In an interview published in the February, 1981, issue of the *Air Force Times*, Dr. Robert F. Murray, who headed the National Academy of Sciences team, said that such studies had not been done. He noted that his team had intended that any restrictions on flight training be temporary until the studies could be completed. Dr. Murray disputed most of the earlier evidence. He said that both of the Air Force Academy cadets who collapsed and died had been recovering from influenza. He also said that the red blood cells of people who have sickle cell trait change to a sickle shape after death. Therefore, autopsy studies of blood cells such as those done on the army recruits at Fort Bliss did not prove that sickle cell trait caused their deaths.

That year, the Air Force Academy dropped its ban on accepting people with the sickle cell trait.

In 1985 Vance Marchbanks received a letter from an old friend who was a colonel in the Air Force Medical Corps. The letter said, in part: "I am enclosing for your information a copy of the memorandum for the Service Secretaries (Army, Navy, Air Force) regarding 'Lifting Duty Restrictions Based on the Presence of Hemoglobin SA in Military Personnel.' I would like to think that this puts to rest once and for all the issue of sickle-cell trait in military occupations. This directive is a most significant step in the right direction."

It was important, because people with sickle cell trait can now serve their country as pilots, divers, paratroopers, and commandoes if they so choose.

5

HOPE FOR
THE FUTURE

Doctors have found many ways to treat the symptoms of sickle cell anemia. However, none of these treatments corrects the basic problem: the red blood cells that sickle when they are starved for oxygen. Some researchers are now trying to alter the genes that produce these defective cells. Other researchers are seeking a substance that will stop or reverse the sickling process.

In the early 1970s, a number of anti-sickling agents were tested extensively. Some of the more successful chemicals appeared to be urea, sodium cyanate, potassium cyanate, and glyceraldehyde. Normal testing procedure would have been to try the more promising substances on laboratory animals to see how effective each chemical was in controlling the sickling process. These animals would then have been killed and their tissues examined under a microscope to determine whether the compounds were causing unwanted damage to desirable cells in the body or producing other serious side effects.

However, these tests on animals could not be performed, because sickle cell anemia occurs only in human beings. So all tests had to be performed *in vitro.*

IN VITRO TESTING

In vitro means "outside of a living organism" (such as a person or a laboratory animal). For *in vitro* procedures, researchers collect red blood cells from a person with sickle cell anemia and place them in a laboratory dish. Various compounds are then put into the dish so that the laboratory workers can observe the effect of each substance on the living cells.

The most promising anti-sickling agents were tried on people who had sickle cell anemia. Since the chemicals had not been tested on laboratory animals to determine whether they caused harmful effects, researchers proceeded very carefully in order to avoid harming the subjects.

Some anti-sickling compounds appeared promising, causing the red cells to hold more oxygen. An increased capacity to hold oxygen decreased the tendency of such cells to tighten into the tough, sickle shapes that block blood flow through an individual's tiny veins or capillaries. Researchers hoped the anti-sickling compounds would lessen the misery felt by patients during pain crises or prevent the sickling process entirely.

However, some of the compounds that looked hopeful in laboratory trials were found to have little or no beneficial effects when tried on human beings. Others seemed to help but had side effects. Sometimes these side effects were minor, causing only indigestion or mild pain. Others were serious, damaging vital organs, such as the heart or kidneys. Some

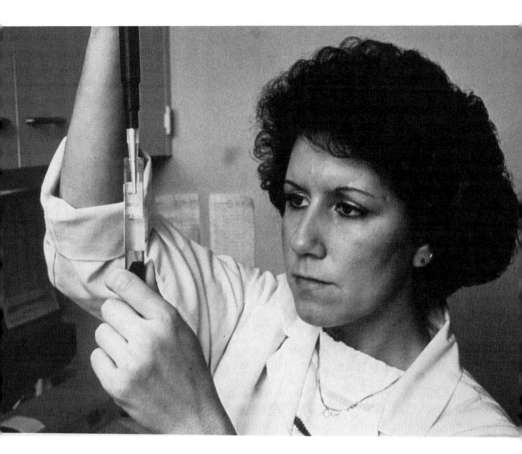

*A researcher carrying out an in vitro procedure
in the search for a cure for sickle cell anemia*

compounds poisoned a patient's entire system when given in doses large enough to be effective. Gradually these tests of anti-sickling compounds were abandoned.

Even though this work produced no usable anti-sickling treatment, researchers learned more about

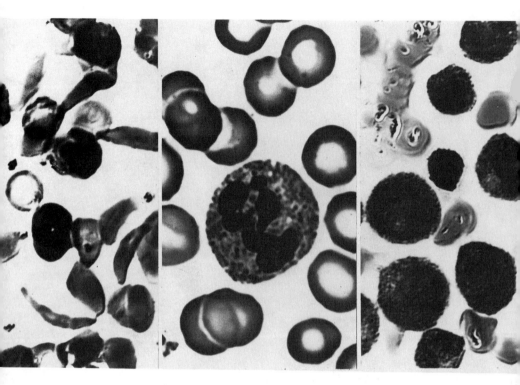

Comparisons of normal and diseased blood:
left, *sickle cell anemia, showing smaller red blood cells*
that are noticeably deformed; center, *normal blood;*
right, *leukemia diseased blood with abnormally high*
number of darker and larger white cells that multiply
cancerously throughout the blood system.

what was happening within the red blood cells during
the sickling process.

BONE MARROW TRANSPLANTS

Another line of research, pursued over the past ten
years, shows more promise: transplanting bone mar-

row from one person to another. Bone marrow produces hemoglobin, and healthy bone marrow transplants to a person with sickle cell anemia will, theoretically, produce healthy hemoglobin. Production of healthy hemoglobin goes beyond treatment of symptoms, even if it doesn't deal with the defective genes themselves. However, such transplants are risky and can produce serious complications.

Doctors at the University of Chicago Medical Center first reported using a bone marrow transplant for sickle cell treatment in 1982. The patient was an eight-year-old girl who had been diagnosed with sickle cell anemia when she was two years old. From the ages of four to eight she averaged one or two hospital admissions each year because of pain crises.

In September, 1982, she also developed an acute form of leukemia, a serious and often fatal blood disease. It was then that her doctors decided to try a bone marrow transplant as a way to attack both of these disorders. The doctors' aim was to suppress the leukemia and convert the girl's sickle cell anemia into sickle cell trait, the latent form of the disease.

The child's four-year-old brother had sickle cell trait, and the doctors determined that he would be a suitable donor. In all transplant cases, the human body tries to fight off—or reject—cells that come from another person, even when that person is a close relative and considered to be a suitable donor. To overcome this problem of rejection, doctors used a number of measures that are routine for such transplants. These included radiation treatments and strong drugs that suppress the person's immune system.

Bone marrow was taken from the girl's brother

and transplanted into her body. Her immune system was then suppressed to avoid rejection of the bone marrow. She also was given penicillin to treat the pneumonia she developed because her immune system had been so greatly suppressed.

The operation was successful, and the girl had no further pain crises and has remained in complete remission from leukemia. Electrophoretic scans of the child's blood revealed that the level of hemoglobin S—the kind that produces the sickling effect—fell from 78 percent at the time when the acute leukemia was diagnosed to 20 percent soon after the transplant. Hemoglobin A, the normal kind, had not been detectable before the transplant. It rose to 62 percent one month after the bone marrow infusion.

Since that pioneering work with bone marrow transplant, fifteen other patients have been treated in this way. Three of the fifteen also had another life-threatening disease, such as leukemia. All fifteen of these patients survived the procedure.

Researchers believe that bone marrow transplants must be severely limited to those people who have life-threatening or near-life-threatening conditions such as leukemia, because there are serious dangers that the body will reject the bone marrow in spite of all precautions. Death from rejection is known to occur in about 20 percent of all transplant cases.

FETAL HEMOGLOBIN

Another promising new way to treat sickle cell anemia involves stimulating the body's production of hemoglobin F. Small amounts of this hemoglobin, produced in the fetus before birth, remain in the body after a child is born. Fetal hemoglobin differs from regular hemoglobin, because it contains gamma globulin chains instead of beta chains. For this reason, the fetal hemoglobin is not affected by the genetic defect that causes sickle cell disease. An increase in the level of this fetal hemoglobin decreases the sickling effect in the patient's blood.

Researchers say that they could minimize the most severe symptoms of sickle cell anemia if they could stimulate the patient's body to replace over 20 percent of the red blood cells with others that contain hemoglobin F. To do this, they need a drug that will cause the body to continue to produce fetal hemoglobin indefinitely instead of only during the prenatal stage.

In 1990 a team of researchers at the National Institutes of Health in Bethesda, Maryland, reported on tests they made with a substance called hydroxyurea that appears to accomplish this. Ten patients with sickle cell anemia were given hydroxyurea for three months. In seven of the ten patients, the levels of fetal hemoglobin increased dramatically. The remaining three did not respond to treatment.

All the people used in the test had severe, long-standing complications from sickle cell anemia, such as recurrent pain crises, chronic bone pain, and leg ulcers. Eight were men and two were women, and the group ranged in age from twenty-two to forty-two years old. Each took the hydroxyurea by mouth. All were closely monitored for side effects.

Patients were considered responsive to treatment if the amount of hemoglobin F in their bodies doubled during the tests. The increase of hemoglobin in the seven people who responded successfully to the treatment ranged from that level up to a tenfold increase in one person. It was thought that the three who did not respond to treatment might be helped by prolonged use at higher doses, but additional tests have not yet been reported. There is a significant problem with hydroxyurea: it is toxic to bone marrow and cannot be used in children.

GENETIC STIMULATION

What the hydroxyurea appeared to do—for reasons that scientists do not fully understand—is stimulate the gene that produces hemoglobin F so that the sickle cell sufferer has a source of hemoglobin unaffected by the genetic defect that causes sickling. If additional tests confirm these original results, the use of hydroxyurea would give researchers a way to treat the root cause of sickle cell disease.

Although hydroxyurea is promising for some patients, it causes toxic side effects in others. A lower dose that would still produce the desired results was needed. Researchers found that they can get the required effect by combining hydroxyurea with another compound, a growth hormone called erythropeletin. This combination uses a lower dose of hydroxyurea and produces a more rapid increase in the fetal hemoglobin than that obtained by using the hydroxyurea alone at its highest recommended dose.

In 1992, scientists found that a drug they were studying as a cancer therapy might turn out to be a treatment for sickle cell anemia and certain other blood disorders. This drug is already used to treat certain rare metabolic disorders in children and is known to be nontoxic, even at high doses. At this point, the studies of the usefulness of this drug in treating sickle cell anemia are preliminary, but there is high interest and much ongoing research.

Promising results in stimulating production of fetal hemoglobin have been obtained with the chemical called butyrate (pronounced BUTE-eh-rate). A simple fatty acid that is found in the body, and in certain foods, butyrate stimulated the production of fetal hemoglobin when tried in a pilot study involving six patients at the Children's Hospital Oakland Research Institute in Oakland, California, in 1992.

Butyrate had no effect on hemoglobin when eaten in foods. So researchers prepared a form of the compound called arginine butyrate that could be infused into a patient's bloodstream. After two or three weeks of this infusion, the patients' bodies increased production of fetal hemoglobin by 6 percent in the lowest case, up to 45 percent in the highest result.

More testing is needed, but Dr. Susan Perrine, the study's lead scientist at the Oakland Children's Hospital, states: "I think this has potential to become a definitive treatment of the underlying disease, as opposed to today's palliative treatment of symptoms to support the patient after complications arise."

Other researchers have dubbed the work with hydroxyurea and butyrate "exciting potential therapies" and said that they are "cautiously optimistic" that these methods of treatment will give them important new tools in the struggle to find better ways to help people who suffer from sickle cell disease.

GENE THERAPY

Another method of treating inherited diseases is still so new that scientists cannot yet speculate about the effect it may have on sickle cell anemia. Called human gene therapy, this method shows great promise in preliminary trials against another inherited disease.

Human gene therapy involves actually altering an individual's genes in the laboratory so that the new ones do not have the defect found in the genes the person had at the time of his or her birth. The gene alterations are brought about by specially created viruses genetically engineered in a laboratory.

Red blood cells are removed from the patient. In the laboratory, these cells are then infected with the virus designed to carry a gene that will correct the condition. The virus is called a vector, or carrier, because it can carry the human genes and insert them into the person's chromosomes without causing a harmful infection. The engineered virus had been genetically altered so that it carried a copy of the human gene for the missing enzyme in the patient's blood. These genetically altered cells, now able to make the normal enzyme, grew and multiplied in the laboratory until they numbered in the billions. They were then injected back into the body where they began correcting the condition caused by the original defective genes.

Although this technique has not yet been tried on a person with sickle cell anemia, it was used successfully in 1990 on a woman who had another condition caused by a defective gene. The woman had inherited an incomplete gene that crippled her immune system so that it no longer protected her from chronic infections. As a result, such infections would have eventually killed her.

Blood was removed from the patient, exposed to the specially engineered virus, and put back into her body. The engineered genes replaced the defective ones just as the doctors had hoped that they would, providing a successful treatment for an inherited condition.

Since gene therapy worked to correct an inherited illness caused by a defect in a single gene, scientists speculate that it will also be effective against other such conditions, including muscular dystrophy, Huntington's disease, cystic fibrosis, and sickle cell anemia.

Gene therapy also offers hope that medical science may be able to produce laboratory animals that can be used to test new medications for sickle cell anemia. A team of researchers at the National Institutes of Health recently inserted sickle cell anemia genes into mice. The researchers hope to create a new strain of these animals that will have sickle cell disease. This new strain of mice would then be used for tests that now must be performed in vitro or on human beings.

DECADES OF PROGRESS

Much has changed in humankind's knowledge about sickle cell disease during the nearly nine decades that have passed since Dr. James Herrick peered into his microscope and saw the peculiar, sickle-shaped cells in the blood of a West Indian man. In the United States it is no longer the rule that 30 percent of the children born with sickle cell anemia must die during early childhood.

Testing of newborn babies alerts parents and doctors to the presence of sickle cell disease. One single medical practice, the use of penicillin to prevent infection in babies, greatly extends the lives of people with sickle cell anemia.

The comprehensive sickle cell program, begun in 1972, alerts parents to the nature of sickle cell disease and helps them cope with cases that appear within their families. Although children will continue to know the sharp, sudden, internal pains that occur when their body tissues cry out for oxygen, they now know the cause of such pains and what can be done to alleviate them.

Above all, children such as Janet, Jacque, Bettina, and Carrie, with sickle cell anemia, can hope that the day will soon come when modern medical research will conquer their illness, as it has conquered so many others. When that day comes, the disease that traveled to the United States over three-and-a-half centuries ago will become only a memory instead of the nightmare that it has been for so many years.

ASSOCIATIONS AND CENTERS

National Association For Sickle Cell Disease, Inc.
3345 Wilshire Boulevard, Suite 1106
Los Angeles, CA 90010
Telephone: (213) 936-7205
Toll-Free: (800) 421-8453

The Sickle Cell Anemia Foundation of Greater
  New York, Inc.
127 West 127th Street, Room 421
New York, NY 10027
Telephone: (212) 865-1500

Howard University Center for Sickle Cell Disease
2121 Georgia Avenue, NW
Washington, DC 20059
Telephone: (202) 806-7930

Comprehensive Sickle Cell Center
University of South Alabama
College of Medicine
Department of Pediatrics
2451 Fillingim Street
Mobile, AL 36617
(205) 471-7099

Comprehensive Sickle Cell Center
University of California
San Francisco General Hospital
1001 Potrero Avenue, Rm. 6J-5
San Francisco, CA 94110
(415) 821-5169

Comprehensive Sickle Cell Center
Boston City Hospital
818 Harrison Avenue, FGH-2
Boston, MA 02118
(617) 424-5727

Comprehensive Sickle Cell Center
Wayne State University School of Medicine
Children's Hospital of Michigan
3901 Beaubien Boulevard
Detroit, MI 48201
(313) 577-1546

Comprehensive Sickle Cell Center
Montefiore Hospital Medical Center
Rosenthal Main
111 East 210th Street
Bronx, NY 10467
(212) 920-6310

Comprehensive Sickle Cell Center
College of Physicians & Surgeons
Columbia University
630 West 168th Street
New York, NY 10032
(212) 305-5808

Comprehensive Sickle Cell Center
Duke University Medical Center
Box 3934 Morris Building
Durham, NC 27710
(919) 684-3724

Comprehensive Sickle Cell Center
Children's Hospital Research Foundation
Elland and Bethesda Avenues
Cincinnati, OH 45229
(513) 559-4543

Comprehensive Sickle Cell Center
The Children's Hospital of Philadelphia
34th Street & Civic Center Boulevard
Philadelphia, PA 19104
(215) 596-9500

Comprehensive Sickle Cell Center
Meharry Medical College
Department of Pediatrics
1005 D.B. Todd Jr. Boulevard
Nashville, TN 37208
(615) 327-6763

FOR FURTHER READING

BOOKS

Callender, Sheila. *Blood Disorders: The Facts*. New York: Oxford University Press, 1985. (An overview of blood diseases.)

Edelstein, Stuart J. *The Sickled Cell: From Myth to Molecules*. Cambridge, Mass.: Harvard University Press, 1986. (General information on sickle cell disease.)

Linde, Shirley. *Sickle Cell: A Complete Guide to Prevention and Treatment*. New York: Pavilion, 1972. (An easy-to-understand approach to the subject.)

Scott, Roland B., ed. *Advances in the Pathophysiology, Diagnosis, and Treatment of Sickle Cell Disease*. New York: Alan R. Liss, 1982. (Technical information on sickle cell disease.)

Serjeant, Graham R. *Sickle Cell Disease*. New York: Oxford University Press, 1985. (Mostly technical, but some easier-to-understand information.)

Whitten, Charles F., and John F. Bertles, eds. *Sickle Cell Disease*. New York: New York Academy of Sciences, 1989. (Technical information on the subject.)

PAMPHLETS

How to Help Your Child to "Take It in Stride." Pamphlet available from the National Association for Sickle Cell Disease, Inc., 3345 Wilshire Boulevard, Suite 1106, Los Angeles, CA 90010.

Management and Therapy of Sickle Cell Disease. U.S. Department of Health and Human Services, Public Health Service, National Institutes of Health, Bethesda, MD—NIH Publication No. 89-2117, Revised 1989. Booklet available from the Superintendent of Documents, U.S. Government Printing Office, Washington, DC 20402.

What's All This Talk About Sickle Cell? Pamphlet available from Howard University Center for Sickle Cell Disease, 2121 Georgia Avenue, NW, Washington, DC 20059.

INDEX

ABOUT THE AUTHOR

George Beshore has written about scientific and environmental subjects for newspapers, magazines, and the federal government for over thirty years. He is the author of two other books published by Franklin Watts, *Science in Ancient China* and *Science in Early Islamic Culture*. Mr. Beshore is now a full-time freelance writer, living in Alexandria, Virginia.